HUMAN ACHIEVEMENTS

BIRDS
LLC

Human Achievements

Lauren Hunter

BIRDS, LLC | MINNEAPOLIS, NEW YORK, RALEIGH

Birds, LLC
Minneapolis, New York, Raleigh
www.birdsllc.com

Cover designed by Zoe Norvell
Interior designed by Michael Newton

Cover & interior art by Dara Cerv

Author photo by Jessica Q. Stark

Library of Congress Cataloging-in-Publication Data:
Hunter, Lauren
Human Achievements/Lauren Hunter
Library of Congress Control Number: 2016960885

First Edition, 2017
ISBN-13: 978-0-9914298-5-1
Printed in the United States of America

HUMAN ACHIEVEMENTS

I think it's hard to write poetry
look how often it doesn't work for those
who should have succeeded
but I also think it's not easy
to take poison climb mountain tops
or swim across the English Channel
and yet all these are human achievements
that's why I dare one more time

Halina Poświatowska

disco affirmation

give me
the good lies
and no shit
i've got magic
in my veins—sweat silks
in a subway tunnel
your apartment on fire
my feet on the pavement
i feel love

hold you in his arms till you can feel his disease

a life story told in karaoke
a blues of stained jeans and gold bangles
of mcdonald's breakfast and stonewashed jeans
i just want to fling my hands into a crowd and pull them tight around me

i just want to whine into a microphone wrapped in furs
let's talk luxury—this bold horn section for one
and the hired soundtrack symphony
can't blame a girl for exploding
or dancing when there's no cause

gorgeous

by the cut of my eye i saw it
a flash and by green i swear it winked at me
over the swing of its wing where i
launched the pin
missing by not quite enough
it shuddered at me and balked
biting *adore* from the tip of my tongue

and to its defense (boundless a malted
crick in the teeth) i fall but not before
gripping the rope of its hair in my palms
psalmsing loudly over

the fear the fear

but my defeat is effortless
a wallow in knee-deep orange gorgeous muck
and on the other side it's easy for
my breath to wander   heavy maybe
the air is thick but never warm like this
renaissance thank not

that i roam on all fours no silent
admission of my actual betterment the glow
sparkling from my belly close
to the grass where the beautiful monster
bows to my consequence

i am bound by nothing and anything
free i feel i blow nights over this and rest
in the safety of a pushing mother these urges
i bear this unremarkable bloom

awakening

would walk for miles to your ocean
to be the waves beating at your shores

forgive my ordinary notions promises
i don't intend to keep i just like

to look i just like to know i could
the only thing i am interested in is not you

your not-hand being mine or anyone's
that girl i touched in the airport the sparks

burning over my skin my teeth electric i ate
a sandwich and never blinked i can sleep

anywhere i bleed deep into the sheets
and bleach and bleach and bleach i plug

my ears and wait read the breeze i
overdeveloped the film and can't go home again

HUMAN ACHIEVEMENT: BOOKLOVE

for our survival for our survival for our survival for our survival we build an arsenal of books, I pour too much diet coke and flood the keyboard, thinking of the spot on park avenue that saved my new york life. FOR OUR SURVIVAL, we build paper forts and ditch digital format. I gave up my discman to make more room for novels, and I faked no fear of heights to fill the dream hole of belonging to shakespeare and laughing in the stacks. is this real. I pinch myself all the time, and my fingertips slide through the skin. good times, swell times, strong voices entering the folds, and one line will do it: *it is the ringing phone that keeps beige horses from dragging me into sleep.* and for our survival we are only slightly patient. the grey horse becomes internet explorer and says I can't listen to any more prince. for our survival, I turn on the lamp and look busy. I bite a savage tongue. I wait and fill word documents.

HUMAN ACHIEVEMENT: SAD SACK

I go to the tattoo parlor wearing a frown. I tell the man: *I want to always remember feeling this sadness.* I've been recounting missing hands for days. he doesn't buy that my sorrow goes that deep and refuses the ink. in my fury, I sharpie his windshield with obscenities. I'm on several warpaths: irresponsible companies, careful bartenders, empty shells of former selves. I count my old friends and line them up against the garden wall: crack, crack, crack. I beg each one to bash in my knees with a pole—no one will, though I see a spark like desire in g's eye. I kick my friends with my still-solid legs, and they just stand there. am I a ghost. I run to the phone booth and try to weep. *even your tear ducts don't believe you*, I say to myself. I use my sharpie to write four phone numbers on the glass. two of them are mine. I walk back home and wait for your call. after 10, I go see my friends, who keep forgiving me. I come home drunk and erase the message without playing it. I never call back, because I don't want to bore you. and also, I don't have the number.

HUMAN ACHIEVEMENT: SUNDAY

because it's sunday and I'm dead, or dead-like, waiting for a sunlight-filtered ghost to slip in and raise the hairs on my arm, I say, to no one in particular, *friends, my dear beauties of the seas, can I call you mermaids, sirens, sharks, stingrays, you gorgeous giant squid of it—good morning.* just a speech to my mirror to keep the chords in order—sunday, monk-like, I swallow my voice almost completely. but that my devotion is to my disease, I would love to sing to you bright monday morning: *dears, wasn't that something, tramping through the snowdrifts from wreck to wreck, burying the smallest bodies.* I've been rereading letters and typing musically. if I'm asleep, then I'm crying for the things I've lost; if I'm awake, I don't know what they are.

april fools

april always comes along
to ruin my life
so i'm in love with martin landau
in north by northwest
he's annoying and ruthless
and has the clearest blue eyes

i'm sorry for all failures
mine and otherwise
i can take the heat

monstrous applause always raises my lips

but what i want
is so much easier
than adoration
i want to make breakfast
and savor it with you

to laugh lying in grass we could never own
mirror interviews via late night skype
and i knew you as a child
the very it of it

there's no more fight
in my valley we pacifists
go on burning our own homes
to show you how it's done

on wings and on fire
missing and missing

the thing is
we're already unhappy here

i, too, dream

of where i am as where i'm supposed to be
how i now saunter up to strangers and friends alike muttering *look into my heart*
holding my ribcage open with my own steady hands

when the ufo crashed into our backyard pool and the other kids scattered
but i pressed against the sliding glass door like
and what like i've not chased boys around the cul-de-sac with knives
like i didn't mean it like i didn't not mean it   i want to tell about the most
idyllic childhood traumas the crash and summertime ghosts and that time
i wanted a bee for a pet   how about these ides asshole   i am fond
of misplacing my anger on you dredging up the drowned barn and each bloated
cow to lay on your hearth   a sweet rot and gifts   go on and scold me
i'm listening   i'm amused by every single one of my faults

HUMAN ACHIEVEMENT: THE FIRST DAY OF MY LIFE

on the first day of my life, I wake up to a radiator screeching *work it girl*. my late dream is a waiting room, and we are counting our turns in the elevator to the testing. this is pointless because we will all pass. but I love the turquoise vinyl chairs and the blue florescent lights and the air that holds a faint cotton candy flavor. on my tongue, is my tongue.

...

in my last life, I awoke to my muscles screeching to a halt and all my insides saying, *don't you ever dare*. I can't, and so don't, get up. I linger in a pit until it's quiet, then turn my radio madness on. I fall asleep to the rhythm of my skin buzzing everywhere, grinding my teeth into salt.

...

then on the first day of my life, I'm in an office that pretends it is familiar. I twitch like an imposter. I lie and say I have no qualms about this work. I hide my past lives and all those paper cuts in the bottom right drawer. everyone punches me right in the throat, but I haven't the time to be wounded or sane.

...

on the first day of my life, I pretend I am just like everyone else and so sorry, and I think they believe me. I'm pretty sure I've been electrocuted twice this morning; if I've forgotten my head, I'm unaware. all of my skin is recovery fresh and radioactive. but I look at that girl I am, that is a ghost, and I tell her to go on— we've still got work to do.

loose lips

comes hard and goes easy like march and other platitudes
i have decided to spend the summer with rats
when i press my palms completely together the world keeps spinning   nothing changes

i would follow your heels to the edge of the earth
and if you walked off i'd follow there too

we grow stronger than our allergies to each other   melodrama with horns
i honor you like the perfect hand on my breast
do we breathe do we age do we drive our backs into fences
that old horse comes around singing *neigh neigh*

honey do what you want

they'll tell me how to feel about you
and how long to hold your hand
how tight

what you said with your big mouth

with your corporate heart on its knees in the bathroom
the cotton ball in the back of our throats
that we keep kissing but can't get out

this way to love   love
to the narrow stairway in the ground
this is where i keep my feeling
stockpiled like canned salmon in a bunker

so i've gnawed the sides of my tongue off
but it works   listen babe we've got
all the time and most of the words

been sh-sh-shaking my whole life
dry kindling suffocating a spark

HUMAN ACHIEVEMENT: CYBORG

when they program our phones to our brains, I want to be sure they give my eye camera the right prescription—full on focus like my eyes can't do. I fell in love because I saw you clearly, saw the yellow house where this inevitably ends, with your blood on my hands. you're a monster in reverse, a peach tree beginning to bloom. take me under and tangled in roots. I revolt at being buried, but do love arms so.

HUMAN ACHIEVEMENT: TO BE FREE

when I wake up, I look the day right in the eye and tell it to go fuck itself, because that is how I feel. if it is beautiful, and even if I feel good, I know somehow I will be held responsible for this. the only way I get out of bed these days is to take my phone and queue up videos of you, talking about things that you love. I laugh around my toothbrush, waiting for my right leg to wake up. what if I go back to bed. it's a condition of my disease, that I see myself hit by a car and don't feel anything. it's like a love tap. I need to exfoliate so many layers of skin to get to what you're asking. the question is about phantom limbs and also sleep paralysis. because that demon on my chest stole my soul, I mean the thing I am missing is my heart, and I can't find it anywhere. is the panic the phantom limb. is the arm the shovel or the knife. because there isn't time. but I am impressed, I am inspired, I am incited. I will buy what you are selling; I am making you something to buy.

having a tooth removed with you

like winning the lottery as you fall into a coma or
literally having your face ripped off mid-kiss i keep
telling myself to change but still hate myself when
i am bleeding i consider it a failure of my humanity
which unlike yours is more than human i tell you
i am batman but unlike my heroic alter-ego i have
real superpowers not just an axe to grind and a really
impressive bank account   maybe i spend
the time on my hands doing nothing
but what if i wake up tomorrow
and it's 1962 again   i'd love to say
i'd stand up swinging but look at my record
mostly i'm dead asleep and even not
tired and useless
the terrible things i say about my unborn children   did i mention
my neck has been bleeding for days and yet nothing
somehow i am the voice that insists i *be reasonable*
and it is killing me   look
my hands are shaking this page is torn my heart is out of warranty
please return to point of purchase

selina kyle's apartment

i'm a woman who wants things i'm a woman
with desires and lists of desires and one of those lists
is labeled LIFE GOALS and another the pages of my autobiography
some mapping evidence and some consequence lists
coming out my ears and yet nothing crossed off
except me   i'm collecting indignant rage these days i'm building
mini monuments to revenge and desire and
groceries like this too-pink apartment filled with stuffed animals
i've never desired like the impulse to destroy your own home
because you deserve it   i wanna go to a pity party where
someone else is the guest of honor i have nothing to say because i don't
know anything because girls who know things get thrown out of windows
and eaten by their own cats   i think it is a miracle
every day my veins don't just burst and the walls stay so white
each day that i don't come around with paintbrushes and shoe polish making the world
look like me   an indeterminate number of gifts
have been given and lost welcome home

she's very good at the gentle and
she's very skilled at the narrow and she's very good and warm and nice and
blood blood blood it's easy to forget

when the gloves come off (or on) and a woman is furious when a woman
decides to express her anger the sex appeal of a woman who doesn't give a shit
and yet suddenly desires skin-tight clothing a woman with nothing left
to hide she destroys things because she feels destroyed duh anger
is so addictive and acidic pitiful and pink apartment encouraging all the rage allowed

wall vs girl

WAIT

WHAT THAT WALL THERE SAID OF ME IT SAID TWO THINGS
ACTUALLY SAID LOVE AND BORE HER BORE HER HEAD UNDER
DEEP SOIL IT SAID

THE WALL HAS A MOUTH AND HANDS NO EYES BUT FEARS
ME IT SAYS FINE LET'S FIGHT IT SAYS BRING IT SAYS BORE HER
HEAD UNDER SHALLOW WATER IT SAID

WHOLED HER YES HOLD HER BACK STILL FEED AND FEAR HER
LOVE HER AND BEAR HER BURY HER HEAD DEEP IT SAID TWO
THINGS ACTUALLY

HUMAN ACHIEVEMENT: ELEGY FOR MY POETRY

last night at a birthplace, recall that room wherein a thing was born and set aflame and died in a few moments. life sores. sulks and shudders. in my dreams I am all the moms, and my babies are out of control and running around like invisible animals. I sew up the broken doctor while his wife, under the blade, is fluidless. her baby like a well-trained bike chain in her belly. why am I the only one awake now. I can't take the pressure. my baby's head on my thigh, *there, there, there*. my thoughts can no longer be controlled nor can I, do you hear me. my hands are strong, strong pink fingernails like can scratch down a brick wall. are you l i s t e n i n g. this morning, as my back broke, all my words died. I saw them float smokily through a distant chimney, and my mouth was dry. I pretended to be the child that has to be told:

you're all alone, babe, everyone's gone on.

well, I will wait. I'm not patient; I'm stubborn. I fold into my own fist, which can be jammed in my pocket, down my throat,   in any small drawer or glove compartment. whitewash my sleep and make those lies golden; why can't I whatever I want. there's no destination; there's no waking then walking. I can live this day forever and lead those babies home but I'll never be there with my love on a plate saying *I am for you and filled—*

HUMAN ACHIVEMENT: THE GIRL I MISS

at one-thirty am, one climbs over me in a rush, tripping on my sleeping feet. she is gone an hour before I return to sleep alone but find instead a mosquito hell-bent on sucking me dry. swollen little love bites on my forehead, my fingers and cheeks. no wonder she has left me, not as alone as I'd like. the bug whines in my ear each time I slide toward unconsciousness. so instead I read and mutter curses. I am alone, right. the woman in this novel is so clueless; are we always so blind. I hate blighted love stories because I read to escape my own petty life. at four am I think my head is finally heavy as I offer up my feet to the vampire, completely indifferent to what I may awaken as.

...

she calls me on the telephone and is walking around town. she tells me she thinks she is near my abandoned apartment. I think hopefully of my collecting mail and micheladas. I keep putting myself apart and blaming everyone else. these days I zombie in and don't talk on the phone. she reminds me of the times I was fun. I am congested and my jaw is swollen. I only wish I had been in a fight.

. . .

I am eating soup in silence while my phone buzzes. I joke about my mother, who I miss. my girls get together and maybe think on me. I have floated out on the ether and am nobody. my body fails and the rest is shutting down. automatic programs send a psychic message to the girl I miss. no message but I like the missed call. my whole self beams, *soon*. I try to pretend the mountains are molehills. I tell myself I'll be normal and pleased. I pretend that I want to return to myself.

i am warm and powerful

this happens when i am between asleep
and you   when my hair is wet
call me hurricane i answer to anything

these warm waters feed
my frenzy   be kind to me   it has
no bearing on your survival
put me in the car i need
constant motion   i am a still
still thing   i need to be pressed

back inside my borders
everynight i come
with only these instructions
expect southern weather

révolutionnaire

i bite off each finger
one-by-one i'm looking
to accuse less lay
the blame game in
an 8-foot grave keep
my hands busy and
my face uncovered
indigestion and nerves
have got nothing on
my appetite i woke
up one morning
and swallowed the sun
nothing to be done about it

do not try to do too much with your own hands.

you held the body in your hands—they were strong suddenly and your tears
were arrows in my side   we watched you work   a barbarian
surgeon poking and shaking your sister awake   you shouted *breathe* and
your aunt burst in with knives   they reminded you you shouldn't save each
one—some wanted to die and it broke your heart   you said *i'm just trying to
keep alive anyone who wants to be* and you felt the world on your back   panting
fainting   rolling your shoulders down and slouched

do not try to do too much with your own hands.

without two hands feel the world a bit further   on fire and you have no
hose and your mouth is dry   you can climb with your knees but the higher
you go the louder the crying comes   you feel your own flesh burning off
crisping and loose you smell the smoke in your hair   you should close
your eyes and conjure water   you should pray that this desert's oasis is
a soothing balm bath that coats the earth fireproof you can open your eyes and
fall into this illusion just so   bubbles shooting up your nose as you cough
underwater

do not try to do too much with your own hands.

in this bright room are you expressing love   does your slow smile mean desire
or desperation as the book falls from your lap the carpet softening its suicide
do the wrinkles in the red pillowcase mean you cry when you sleep or never
breathe   i watch you walk to me without two hands the carpet caving before
your foot falls   someone's hand at my throat but no arm to swat at

do not try to do too much with your own hands.

perhaps you can't quiet the baby but you can knock out these windows without
a scratch and then we can escape if anything comes in after us   when the hungry
cat nips at our feet i can dance while you grab her your steel hands can hold her
harmless until we lock her outside   you don't feel her claws tear at your fingers
but i can wipe the blood off and your growing hands won't know the difference
you can stir the soup with your finger   you can strangle any stranger
you can push the wrinkle from the carpet—but you just sit   nervous and
shaking   rubbing your monstrous hands in your hands

a little dark hand waving stop in the corner of my eye

i can't stop glancing towards it
what do you want what does anyone want

a spell i have been working on knocks you down every
time you don't think of me perhaps i haven't any talent
but the game is to pretend i'll do you and you do me
you know   hand kissing and the like

my middle finger is becoming a fang   venom gathering in the knuckle
i'm sorry i'm sorry for what

i didn't even recall

all those sad girls i'd been

any occasion in heathers or a single strange night at pete's
and where are those mornings

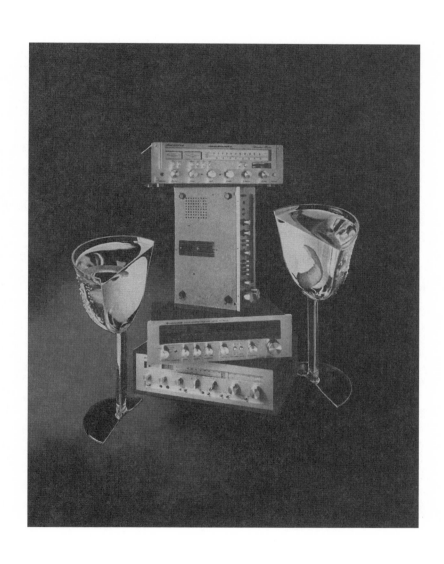

HUMAN ACHIEVEMENT: YULE LOG

it's been four days since you left. I've kept busy, walked into a prism of past lives and scrambled up and out: I'm braver than before. bolder in the eye. it's true—I still worry a little about drinking jack on the sidewalk, but it's cold. shit can't be helped. do you ever wander one bus too far to stand by the sea. I woke up in canarsie, thinking, *drats. drowned rats.* but I get myself to where I can be someone else and linger. draw my posture up and shake hips. I'm not actually able to go home sober and alone. so you decide. my one sure thing is what happens when the horns come in.

HUMAN ACHIEVEMENT: BRUNCHDATE

how about these waterfalls diluting the prairies. they say, *well, stop crying.* I'm impractical so I also begin blowing my nose. nothing ever stops in my head; it just gets frostbitten until I have to amputate. I always save my phantom limbs. so we're going to brunch, and hopefully by a window, and I'll remark on the weather when you ask, *how are you.* an earthquake in my stomach reveals the valley we're ignoring. we are just raining all over this place. I'm ashamed to order the five bloodies I crave. I deny the new york in me but it shows, I hope, if in nothing but my impatience and alcoholism. I didn't dance when you knew me—WE ARE STRANGERS. but our hands will touch too tenderly.

HUMAN ACHIEVEMENT: LATE NITE DELI

a sphinx lion-god winks at me in the late nite deli. it is 3 am. his hands are full of potato chips. sunglasses on his forehead. he looks beached. the sandwich man says, *hello, mi amor*, and hands me a hero. these are not ordinary times. I feel a bit of sleep boring through my eyeball. the sphinx never blinks. his eyes on the back of my head; my bobby pins glowing desert-red. I have a hand on the kombucha fridge, but am not sick. lion-god leans by and places a bag of dark cherries on the counter. and then I am swimming in them; I am choking on swollen pits. he hands me a peach, stone fox fruit. sphinx god has nothing on sleeping this off. a walk in fresh air. a block from home I feel his mouth in my belly and my lungs collapse in the usual way.

HUMAN ACHIEVEMENT: CATCALL

there was a week I walked to yeezus; I lived in new york city. I felt attacked all the time by so many people, too many people, and I turned my headphones up to block unwanted compliments, and I was aching, and the soundtrack was amazing.

to be angry is a thing I have felt, but never learned. I can't express extreme displeasure, can't say no, can't throw the punch that lays it out, but can sully myself with angers fuming, I mean fuming.

and my eyes down because no, and my feet fast because hell no, fists in pockets no, face turned anywhere but no.

I can't get angry because I don't know what comes next—what if it don't go away, if I'm angry all the time. what if suddenly I have to do something about it, have to stand up and call attention, cross the street and run in blazing.

what if no one comes to douse me.

national poetry month

this human-faced lamb
i mean really   clearly
a page is missing from the manual
of should i love it
can you eat it
things that are free can
get a little bulky   and let's
be honest a face only a mother could
i feel free and woke up
this morning i ate a little fruit and
am trying not to vomit

full disclosure: i quit   and then i quit again
so i'm just humoring the letters of the keyboard
that want me to feel in love with them again
i love the phrase going through the motions
because what could be better: i'm out the other side
                                        waving

four minutes ago it was like
poetry: bowls of pink apples and a
yellow tulip reaching for the ceiling fan
which i can really identify with

                                        baby
that ain't the sun   *but i wants it*

i imagine myself eating an apple
without my teeth and by a miracle it works:
i rest my hand on the whole infant apple
sleeping in my belly

what i am reaching for   what the point is
a thousand dolphins dive down at once   bring
me down
like
glass   breaking

poetry is the thing under your tongue
he is kissing to get out   it is the lamp
at five am that blurs your eyes how dare
sweet poetry come in spring is how i feel
dragging my body out of bed   i will just ruin it
i will just use my hands and make a mess of it

the loop

i extend my conscience-calmed
into the void   the answer is *nie*
bite harder because this bread is thick
in a way my skin isn't in a way

occasionally my thoughts and body collide
and make consequence brushing up around
your air so i die by sensation
breathing through my retinas i like to say to myself
i am damage i destruction i like to say

i touch your wrist
and mean it or a *heatwave baby*
on your radio dial this is what i mean
a body not meant to contain
nor control unbearable sways i don't
balance fall off of bikes and plans and
into dark water i hide under the covers and
pray for a blowout or the breakdown want
the plane crashing through the window
busting up my ribcage in the way your face does
heartstrings tangled in my hair do i get
too drunk and cry a lot   that's the kind of question
i wish mattered or have you come this
long way baby have you
broken out and not drowned

no secret how the tears are nonexistent
no secret how my back breaks with longing

HUMAN ACHIEVEMENT: BOOKLIFE

a communion rite we grapple down the hill, wine sloshing down our chins and the toes of our boots in pure agony, pure pleasure, the sign of the moment marked in a photograph I later regret, what was I thinking wearing that dress in fluorescent lights. I bought your book and cried over the first page, then forgot where I left it. this morning (again, in agony) I opened my eyes to an old friend I thought I'd lost and considered the theft if I skipped my day to reunite. by a pleasure I command, my wills are done, or strongly considered in a style not unlike flattery. will nature stop bringing the path to my feet because I am wandering. the love I barely feel can afford no better term than this, be warned.

HUMAN ACHIEVEMENT: INTERNET CRUSH

is this overdoing it. my hands shake at my desk or in my apartment, I've confessed, not much, I'll confess. I've had this theory that the sun rises inside everyone, and I react accordingly. say you've known your whole life exactly what you are and what you want, but they still say no. do you get angry. do you take matters and do something serious with your own hands.

I stay in the house next door to yours—I just walk in like I'm sick and don't know any better, so your neighbors keep me; they don't even know why. I stay away from every window. I daydream about wood paneling on the wall or on the car, and I don't care what else.

if I give up one dream for another. if i follow your brother down the street or to california and shake his hand as if I didn't know.

nothing will ever work without a psychic connection in me, so there's that.

how could you trust a man's eyes more than mine.

the cave of anti-f**r

we crawled inside a sort of comfort bomb
we can be here   we can be here for hours
we can talk about trees we cannot climb
we can avoid the f-word   we can shed
our timid sweaters nothing to look at
but the tops of our own knees   i assume
you are etching the same hieroglyphs
into yours   and i am a warrior you are
too noble to require tears we can beat the
panic back with our bare hands we are
growing tougher than stones

HUMAN ACHIEVEMENT: REDWOODS

what possibilities can there be when I cannot describe the music in my head—
when I cannot hum or play it. the paradox of your green. I often think only on
the profound sadness of life, but I want to turn to joy. want the seconds of burst.
the moments spent enduring the credits to a satisfying cinematic experience.
and you find yourself back in your room, skin crawling with comfort or dis-,
restructuring as you must decide where your life can go from here. I do want to
smash things, but for the moment after when it is silent and I regret it.

...

in dreams I am driving through a forest. this happens every night. winding and resetting, as if I know something. my desires shrink and expand like things I cannot understand; I suppose at a normal rate. what is a want. my eyes keep filling up with tears and I don't know why. the only thing that is safe is if I wear pants, crouched on the couch intent on stabbing me to death, dimma to the tree, dimma to the tree and drowning in things one can chew and swallow.

...

the last time I was drunk, I gave myself a cold—how droll. I love the easy discard of folks. how it is possible I seem indifferent. I am escalating, and I will blow. the spark that spontaneously combusts this sick body that I loathe. the eagerness of vowels. the stench of towels soaked in vomit and bourbon and GLORY GLORY I AM UNFIT HALLELUJAH I AM HOLY AS SIN AND FORGIVE ME ALL FAULTS FORGIVE ME ALL FIGHTS AND THE CONSTANT URGE FOR ESCAPE I AM ALOST.

...

we agreed to write a treatise, build a monument to our loneliness together. sounds like a promise. sounds like not being alone. but was a lie. most things are lies. people speak in pretty languages that are lies. how I love people, because I have told myself to. how a spark across the world moves my hand to my heart, bleeding quietly.

...

I am afraid all the time. I knew the moment I laid eyes on your face something would happen to me. so continues this exhausting struggle to prove something between us. I moved indoors and flaked on friends. made myself a beacon, locked myself in a cocoon for some months. I thought you knew I'd always come back. I thought you knew I was just tired.

love

the sun on your face is electric or
spilling out from within
nostalgic moment you wish you lived in
don't turn around don't let your fingers
slip don't look up or answer the phone
or turn the dial or let the music end don't
move or breathe or scratch the curve of
your left foot this magic isn't
sticking around you won't hold it past
the moment don't count the thousands
of days between this one and the last time
you felt this way don't sit up or take a sip
there is nothing no there is nothing else

be careful with that

tried to make a map out of you
sugar   thought you'd be a simple machine
to manipulate i put my hands on the stars
daily tracking burns down the stairs you have
a lot of nervous intentions we could be dolphins
fireworks like us splashing against the northern sky
what would i want   transparency a little weightlessness
some pools of oil reflecting the entire reach of
up there—out here no trees or rooftops framing the view
and i like that—like if i stood up all of heaven'd crash
down around us   and don't you wish

HUMAN ACHIEVEMENT: RED PHONE

put your number in my phone under *red emergency*, a quick-pull last ditch in case I am in need of awkward and forced human compassion. I'd name you confessor and begin with what I think of you. the wood paneling, the vinyl table top, the shag carpeting. there is a place I have only visited in dreams—it morphs, but is always recognizable and so real I have woken up in panics knowing I can never replicate it perfectly. and now you live there. if that dream is the best thing I ever create, how I hover on the edge of reality from now on.

HUMAN ACHIEVEMENT: PAYPHONE

a woman found half-dead in her brooklyn apartment, no pet to discover the body. broken, heavy and cold, sprawled over the edge of the tub. in movies, they don't let prisoners touch their visitors, and this terrifies me. the thought that for years, maybe, no one touches you gently; no contact, but in violence. I watch too much tv, but I still shudder when a stranger's limb grazes mine and curl too far into myself in a cramped airplane seat, until my body locks itself into an unrecognizable shape. an old man compliments me condescendingly and I smile automatically, then my stomach turns. walking the last block to work, again I vowed to make my life a weapon against white men, but find too many soft spots where I allow myself to be forgiving or kind.

HUMAN ACHIEVEMENT: HEART

I'm interested in what your human heart can hold. I've been championing empathy but lack faith. in my cult, I tell you about a god that will release you into your ultimate potential; here you are with a severe lack of regret. we were on the ocean fighting when I was stabbed in the foot. if I bled, it wasn't appetizing enough, and we washed up, whole and sore. come with me. this way into the warm bath of shame. I'm disinterested in your counter offer; my salvation is good enough for me.

I wash with your eyes, a ghost in my shower, in my window overlooking the alley, smoking out on the fire escape. a pair of sunglasses haunt this shade of gloss. while I sit clipping off pink nails, you are oblivious. when I trip on my suitcase in the dark, a ballerina of brick, you are belittling yourself.

I've no ideas left, but one time a mountain climbed. we've landed in my backyard a hundred times, and this is nothing like my home. we could be forgiven if only, if what. tell us a new story where nothing falls apart.

HUMAN ACHIEVEMENT: GOLDFISH

I buy a goldfish and tell it a secret. every day, when I feed him, I say what it is that I want. I make a thousand wishes on this fish and nothing changes. you came by without warning, and my room was hidden under books and wires. what you were gonna teach me, more importantly, what I've gotta learn. I used to have a capacity and now turn slowly in circles in my room, sobbing and eating the fat off my thighs. I make jokes. I'm particular. I am terrified that if you love me I will owe you something I do not want to give. something I can't readily take back. it's cruel but not to you. it's self-preservation except I started this. I kiss the side of the fishbowl and lie—you are the onliest thing I want, fish.

HUMAN ACHIEVEMENTS

this morning I woke up, and I only wanted to tell the truth. like, last night was a total error in judgement; I am mismanaging my life. I'd hire a replacement if one should apply. there are two girls inside me that have been killed. nonviolently snuffed out by persistent doubt and reckless influence. I am taking my laptop into the tub, I am going to write a letter. to my father, I will say, *forget the medals, I went for medals*. this letter becomes a book titled Continual Failure and Disappointment; my editor will rename it, Human Achievements. my father will say, *the gold, the gold,* but really delights in the calculated leap. I stay quiet and swing low. swing low until the sun sets, and I feel free.

Acknowledgements

Many thanks to the editors of the following publications in which several of these poems first appeared: *pax Americana*; *Words Are Mighty*; *Augury Books*; *Bling that Sings*; *Sink Review*; *Poetry Crush*; *No, Dear*; & *Wreck Park*.

All love & etc. to my incredible family for sustaining me, & for the good times. Neither this book, nor I would exist without their love and encouragement.

A resounding & humble thanks to Dara Cerv for sharing her vision & artwork so generously with this book & its author.

Thank you & thank you to Zoe Norvell & Mike Newton for their work in making this book beautiful.

A multitude of yes to my heartbeats for reminding me I am alive. Special thanks to Lucy Kwon, Christine Kanownik, Paige Taggart, Amy Lawless, Ryan Doyle May, Sampson Starkweather, J Hope Stein, Bianca Stone, Jessica Stark, Emily Withers, Alina Gregorian, & Ben Mirov for their particular part in the life of these poems & this poet.

Thanks to Alex Crowley, Mark Gurarie, Liz Clark Wessel, Emily Brandt, Alex Cuff, Stephanie Berger & Nick Adamski for their invaluable friendship & support.

Thanks & admiration to Mark Bibbins & Rachel Levitsky for their generosity in words, art & counsel.

Supreme gratitude to the Birds, particularly my tireless editor Chris Tonelli, for helping the big dream come true.

!!!

HUMAN ACHIEVEMENT: BOOKLOVE borrows a line from the poem *Beige Horses* by Alina Gregorian.

the cave of anti-f**r is for Taryn Andrews.

HUMAN ACHIEVEMENT: THE GIRL I MISS is for Paige Taggart.

gorgeous is for Mollye Miller & after Bhanu Kapil.

Lauren Hunter is a poet, editor and educator living in Durham, North Carolina. She received her MFA in poetry from The New School and is the managing editor for the experimental translation press Telephone. Lauren is the co-founder/curator of Electric Pumas, an occasional reading series/web presence interested in promoting multimedia art by women. A chapbook, *My Own Fires*, was released by Brothel Books in 2011. *HUMAN ACHIEVEMENTS* is her first book.

Brilliantly, Lauren Hunter lets us step into the shoes of the speaker and wake up. From within these poems we are able to observe; a great longing blooms and walks and reaches out while we look at the world through new eyes. *Human Achievements* explores a contemporary landscape in human isolation—isolation from truth, love, genuine contact and vision. The speaker, locked in the "office that pretends it is familiar," always "channeling out of pleasure to panic," lets herself conceive different scenarios of reality to replace the disappointment of what is there. In this action of transformation there is palpable beauty, joy and wise reflection that I find nothing less than stunning.

— Bianca Stone

Lauren Hunter will pull you all the way through to "the very it of it" with her frightening, sharp, steady, comic, mournful, intimate poems. There's irony around the edges, but it's not a trap. It might be a plea—either way, she shows you what's roiling underneath: "very good and warm and nice and / blood blood blood." Hunter sees something in everything and needs you to see it too. When she says "no shit / i've got magic," go ahead and believe that.

— Mark Bibbins

Every page is a rage spread. Lauren Hunter finds poetry in music, a feminist resistance, and a lyric unsmothering. Her debut *Human Achievements* is full of friends, aching, bleeding, feeling fine, the city, and listening. You know how the right song can change everything, and can be a conduit for energy or rage? "I look the day right in the eye and tell it to go fuck itself." The right song can also turn you into a ghost. She writes: "I linger in a pit until it's quiet, then turn my radio madness on." This book is brilliant and huge-hearted, seeping with duende (if that is even a thing), bleeding with a sort of New York School daily-humor, and finding beauty and self-reflection under a pile of coats while the party is right outside the door. The massive struggle is living just one more day in America. This book is my new favorite soundtrack.

— Amy Lawless

I used to go dancing with Lauren and a couple other friends, once a month, on Friday night, at a party called the Ruff Club on the Lower East Side of New York. Lauren knew the DJ, who would spin doo-wop and oldies until 3 or 4AM. Lauren is an amazing dancer. She's full of subtle gestures and playful turns, yet capable of deep dance-floor introspection and moments of singular righteousness. She knows that dancing is about being with others as much as it is about being alone; she understands how to draw you in with a look, and how to turn mysteriously away into a private groove. I tell you this because most people will never get a chance to experience the catharsis of dancing with Lauren until daybreaks. Most people will never witness the duende, or experience the revelatory calibrations of her spirit. Most people. But not you. You can read this book.

— Ben Mirov